Simple & Delicious

POTATOES

Simple & Delicious
POTATOES

OVER 100 SENSATIONAL RECIPES FOR POTATO LOVERS

This edition published in 2012
LOVE FOOD is an imprint of Parragon Books Ltd

Parragon
Queen Street House
4 Queen Street
Bath BA1 1HE, UK

www.parragon.com/lovefood

ISBN: 978-1-4454-8268-2

Printed in China

Cover Design by Geoff Borin
New Photography by Clive Bozzard-Hill
Home Economy by Valerie Barrett and Carol Tennant

Notes for the Reader
This book uses both metric and imperial measurements. Follow the same units of measurement throughout; do not mix metric and imperial. All spoon measurements are level: teaspoons are assumed to be 5 ml, and tablespoons are assumed to be 15 ml. Unless otherwise stated, milk is assumed to be full fat, eggs and individual vegetables are medium, and pepper is freshly ground black pepper. Unless otherwise stated, all root vegetables should be washed and peeled prior to using.

Garnishes, decorations and serving suggestions are all optional and not necessarily included in the recipe ingredients or method.

The times given are an approximate guide only. Preparation times differ according to the techniques used by different people and the cooking times may also vary from those given. Optional ingredients, variations or serving suggestions have not been included in the time calculations.

Recipes using raw or very lightly cooked eggs should be avoided by infants, the elderly, pregnant women, convalescents and anyone suffering from an illness. Pregnant and breastfeeding women are advised to avoid eating peanuts and peanut products. Sufferers from nut allergies should be aware that some of the ready-made ingredients used in the recipes in this book may contain nuts. Always check the packaging before use.

Contents

Introduction

Potatoes are one of the most common and versatile of all vegetables and are widely used in cuisines all over the world. They are a convenient and economical food and are easy to prepare. Potatoes can be cooked in many different ways to create a tempting range of side dishes, as well as forming the basis for many other delicious recipes, to suit all tastes.

Nutrition

Potatoes are a nutritious, low-fat food packed with starchy carbohydrate for energy. A good source of fibre, they also contain some B vitamins, potassium and vitamin C. Most of the nutrients are found in or under the skin, so keeping the skins on potatoes makes the most of the goodness.

Green or sprouting potatoes (or potatoes with green patches) should be discarded as they contain alkaloids, too much of which can be toxic.

Varieties of Potatoes

There are many varieties of potatoes, offering a wide range of flavours and some different textures. Potatoes are categorized according to their growing season and when they are harvested. They are divided into three potato seasons – new potatoes or earlies (sometimes called first earlies), second earlies and maincrop. Earlies are generally available in stores from April/May–July, and second earlies from around August through to March (but are often obtainable for much of the year). Maincrop are usually available in stores throughout the year with their main season running from around September to May. Potatoes can generally be split into two different kinds according to their cooking qualities – waxy and floury. Waxy potatoes tend to stay firm and keep their shape during cooking, whereas floury potatoes have a drier, fluffier and lighter texture when cooked. Common varieties of waxy potatoes include Charlotte, Maris Peer, Pentland Javelin and Romano. Common varieties of floury potatoes include Estima, Kerr's Pink, King Edward, Maris Piper and Pentland Squire. Some potato varieties such as Cara, Desirée, King Edward, Maris Piper, Romano and Wilja are also considered to be good all-rounders. Jersey Royals, which are regarded as the 'king' of early potatoes, are available for a limited period and are well worth the additional expense for their fine flavour and creamy flesh.

Speciality salad potatoes such as Anya, Pink Fir Apple and Ratte are also obtainable, as are some of the more novel varieties of blue-, black- or purple-fleshed salad potatoes such as Purple Congos.

Sweet potatoes are also a popular choice. They are grown in tropical and subtropical climates and commonly have pink/purple skins with a dense orange, yellow or white flesh with a distinctive sweetish flavour. Sweet potatoes can be cooked by many of the methods that suit standard potatoes.

Buying and Storing Potatoes

When buying potatoes, choose firm, heavy potatoes with a smooth, tight skin and select ones with no obvious spots, blemishes or green patches. Avoid potatoes that are soft, wrinkled or have started to sprout and only buy in quantities that you can cope with. The skins of new potatoes should be flaking off or should rub off easily.

Potatoes should be stored in a cool, dark, dry, airy place. Don't store potatoes in the refrigerator and store them away from strong-smelling foods such as onions. Early and new potatoes are always best eaten soon after they have been lifted to enjoy them at their finest, so buy them in small quantities. Maincrop potatoes, on the other hand, tend to store well under the right conditions.

Potatoes, although often sold in polythene bags in supermarkets, store best and for longer if transferred to paper, cloth or natural fibre bags. Ready-washed potatoes do not keep as well as earthy ones and are best eaten as soon as possible after purchase.

Cooking and Serving Potatoes

Potatoes vary in appearance, taste and texture and some types are better for cooking methods such as boiling or steaming, whereas others are more suited to roasting and baking, and a few varieties are good all-rounders. For example, waxy varieties such as Charlotte and Nicola are good for salads; King Edward, Maris Piper and Wilja are good for mashing; Desirée, King Edward and Maris Piper are ideal for roasting or deep-frying; varieties such as Cara, Estima and Marfona are perfect for baking.

Potatoes are a very versatile ingredient and can be prepared and cooked in numerous ways. They can be left whole, diced, sliced, grated or cut into chunks, wedges, chips, matchsticks or straws. They can be boiled, steamed, baked, roasted, shallow-fried or sautéed, deep-fried (as chips, crisps, straws, ribbons, croquettes, fritters, etc.), microwaved, stir-fried, griddled or barbecued. Cooked potatoes can be mashed, creamed, crushed, used in salads and so on. New potatoes, which tend to have a firm, waxy texture, are ideal for boiling, steaming, sautéing, roasting and using in salads.

New potatoes simply need to be scrubbed or scraped before cooking, whereas old potatoes often need peeling before use (though this depends on how they will be cooked; for example, jacket potatoes are baked with their skins on).

Recipes containing potatoes vary enormously from potato croquettes, cakes and dumplings, to potato soups, salads and sautés. Potatoes also provide a good vehicle for other ingredients, flavours and textures. Tempting potato dishes range from everyday family meals such as fish pie, fish cakes or tortilla, to more sophisticated recipes including gnocchi, dauphinois, rösti, gratins or galettes.

Potatoes also play a key role in classic dishes such as Irish Stew and Bubble & Squeak. Baked, roasted or deep-fried potato skins served with a tasty topping or some delicious dip make an ideal starter or snack to share with friends. Baked potatoes with an appetizing topping or filling create a speedy and nutritious mid-week supper. Potatoes can even be used in some sweet recipes.

1

Soups

Leek & Potato Soup

serves 4–6

55 g/2 oz butter

1 onion, chopped

3 leeks, sliced

225 g/8 oz potatoes, cut into 2-cm/¾-inch cubes

850 ml/1½ pints vegetable stock

salt and pepper

150 ml/5 fl oz single cream, to serve (optional)

2 tbsp snipped fresh chives, to garnish

Melt the butter in a large saucepan over a medium heat, add the onion, leeks and potatoes and sauté gently for 2–3 minutes, until soft but not brown. Pour in the stock, bring to the boil, then reduce the heat and simmer, covered, for 15 minutes.

Transfer the mixture to a food processor or blender and process until smooth. Return to the rinsed-out saucepan.

Heat the soup, season with salt and pepper to taste and serve in warmed soup bowls, swirled with the cream, if using, and garnished with chives.

Roasted Garlic & Potato Soup

serves 4

1 large garlic bulb with large cloves, peeled (about 100 g/3½ oz)

2 tsp olive oil, plus extra for brushing

2 large leeks, thinly sliced

1 large onion, finely chopped

500 g/1 lb 2 oz potatoes, diced

1.2 litres/2 pints chicken or vegetable stock

1 bay leaf

150 ml/5 fl oz single cream

freshly grated nutmeg

fresh lemon juice (optional)

salt and pepper

snipped fresh chives and a sprinkle of paprika, to garnish

Put the garlic cloves in an ovenproof dish, lightly brush with oil and bake in a preheated oven, 180°C/350°F/Gas Mark 4, for about 20 minutes, until golden.

Heat the oil in a large saucepan over a medium heat. Add the leeks and onion, cover and cook for about 3 minutes, stirring frequently, until they begin to soften.

Add the potatoes, roasted garlic, stock and bay leaf. Season with salt (unless the stock is salty already) and pepper. Bring to the boil, reduce the heat, cover and cook gently for about 30 minutes, until the vegetables are tender. Remove the bay leaf.

Allow the soup to cool slightly, then transfer to a blender or food processor and process until smooth, working in batches if necessary. (If using a food processor, strain off the cooking liquid and reserve. Process the soup solids with enough cooking liquid to moisten them, then combine with the remaining liquid.)

Return the soup to the saucepan and stir in the cream and a generous grating of nutmeg. Taste and adjust the seasoning, if necessary, adding a few drops of lemon juice, if using. Reheat over a low heat. Ladle into warmed soup bowls, garnish with chives and paprika and serve.

Chunky Vegetable Soup

serves 6

2 carrots, sliced

1 onion, diced

1 garlic clove, crushed

350 g/12 oz new potatoes, diced

2 celery sticks, sliced

115 g/4 oz closed-cup mushrooms, quartered

400 g/14 oz canned chopped tomatoes

600 ml/1 pint vegetable stock

1 bay leaf

1 tsp dried mixed herbs or 1 tbsp chopped fresh mixed herbs

85 g/3 oz sweetcorn kernels, frozen or canned, drained

55 g/2 oz green cabbage, shredded

freshly ground black pepper

sprigs of fresh basil, to garnish (optional)

Put the carrots, onion, garlic, potatoes, celery, mushrooms, tomatoes and stock into a large saucepan. Stir in the bay leaf and herbs. Bring to the boil, then reduce the heat, cover and simmer for 25 minutes.

Add the sweetcorn and cabbage and return to the boil. Reduce the heat, cover and simmer for 5 minutes, or until the vegetables are tender. Remove and discard the bay leaf. Season to taste with pepper.

Ladle into warmed soup bowls, garnish with basil, if using, and serve immediately.

Broccoli & Cheese Soup

serves 6

25 g/1 oz butter

1 onion, chopped

2 tsp chopped fresh tarragon, plus extra to garnish

450 g/1 lb potatoes, peeled and grated

1.7 litres/3 pints vegetable stock

700 g/1 lb 9 oz broccoli, cut into small florets

175 g/6 oz Cheddar cheese

1 tbsp chopped fresh parsley

salt and pepper

Melt the butter in a large, heavy-based saucepan. Add the onion and cook, stirring occasionally, for 5 minutes, until soft. Add the chopped fresh tarragon to the saucepan with the potatoes, season to taste and mix well. Pour in just enough of the stock to cover and bring to the boil. Reduce the heat, cover and simmer for 10 minutes.

Meanwhile, bring the remaining stock to the boil in another saucepan. Add the broccoli and cook for 6–8 minutes, until just tender.

Remove both pans from the heat, leave to cool slightly, then ladle the contents of both into a blender or food processor. Process until smooth, then pour the mixture into a clean saucepan. Grate the cheese, stir into the pan with the parsley and heat gently to warm through, but do not allow the soup to boil. Ladle into warmed soup bowls, garnish with tarragon and serve immediately.

Indian Potato & Pea Soup

serves 4

2 tbsp vegetable oil

225 g/8 oz floury potatoes, diced

1 large onion, chopped

2 garlic cloves, crushed

1 tsp garam masala

1 tsp ground coriander

1 tsp ground cumin

850 ml/1½ pints vegetable stock

1 fresh red chilli, deseeded and chopped

100 g/3½ oz frozen peas

4 tbsp natural yogurt

salt and pepper

chopped fresh coriander, to garnish

Heat the vegetable oil in a large saucepan. Add the potatoes, onion and garlic and sauté over a low heat, stirring constantly, for about 5 minutes.

Add the garam masala, ground coriander and cumin and cook, stirring constantly, for 1 minute.

Stir in the vegetable stock and red chilli and bring the mixture to the boil. Reduce the heat, cover the pan and simmer for 20 minutes, until the potatoes begin to break down.

Add the peas and cook for a further 5 minutes. Stir in the yogurt and season to taste with salt and pepper.

Pour into warmed soup bowls, garnish with chopped fresh coriander and serve immediately.

Sweet Potato & Apple Soup

serves 6

1 tbsp butter

3 leeks, thinly sliced

1 large carrot, thinly sliced

600 g/1 lb 5 oz sweet potatoes, peeled and diced

2 large, tart eating apples, peeled and diced

1.2 litres/2 pints water

freshly grated nutmeg

225 ml/8 fl oz apple juice

225 ml/8 fl oz single cream

salt and pepper

snipped fresh chives or chopped fresh coriander, to garnish

Melt the butter in a large saucepan over a medium–low heat. Add the leeks, cover and cook, stirring frequently, for 6–8 minutes, or until softened.

Add the carrot, sweet potatoes, apples and water. Season lightly with salt, pepper and nutmeg to taste. Bring to the boil, reduce the heat, cover and simmer, stirring occasionally, for about 20 minutes until the vegetables are very tender.

Allow the soup to cool slightly, then transfer to a blender or food processor and process until smooth, working in batches if necessary. (If using a food processor, strain off the cooking liquid and reserve. Process the soup solids with enough cooking liquid to moisten them, then combine with the remaining liquid.)

Return the puréed soup to the saucepan and stir in the apple juice. Place over a low heat and simmer for about 10 minutes, until heated through.

Stir in the cream and continue simmering for about 5 minutes, stirring frequently, until heated through. Taste and adjust the seasoning, adding more salt, pepper and nutmeg, if necessary.

Ladle into warmed soup bowls, garnish with chives and serve.

Potato & Vegetable Soup with Pesto

serves 6

2 carrots

450 g/1 lb potatoes

200 g/7 oz fresh peas in their pods

200 g/7 oz thin French beans

150 g/5½ oz young courgettes

2 tbsp olive oil

1 garlic clove, crushed

1 large onion, finely chopped

2.5 litres/4½ pints vegetable stock or water

1 bouquet garni of 2 fresh parsley sprigs and 1 bay leaf tied in a 7.5-cm/ 3-inch piece of celery

85 g/3 oz dried small soup pasta

1 large tomato, skinned, deseeded and chopped or diced

Parmesan cheese shavings, to serve

pesto

75 g/2¾ oz fresh basil leaves

1 garlic clove

5 tbsp fruity extra virgin olive oil

salt and pepper

To make the pesto, put the basil leaves, garlic and olive oil in a food processor and process until well blended. Season with salt and pepper to taste. Transfer to a bowl, cover with clingfilm and chill until required.

Peel the carrots and cut them in half lengthways, then slice. Peel the potatoes and cut into quarters lengthways, then slice. Place in a bowl and cover with cold water until ready to use, to prevent discoloration.

Shell the peas. Top and tail the beans and cut them into 2.5-cm/1-inch pieces. Cut the courgettes in half lengthways, then slice.

Heat the oil in a large saucepan or flameproof casserole. Add the garlic and fry for 2 minutes, stirring. Add the onion and continue frying for 2 minutes, until soft. Add the carrots and potatoes and stir for about 30 seconds.

Pour in the stock and bring to the boil. Lower the heat, partially cover and simmer for 8 minutes, until the vegetables are starting to become tender.

Stir in the peas, beans, courgettes, bouquet garni, pasta and tomato. Season and cook for 8–10 minutes, or until tender. Discard the bouquet garni, stir in the pesto and serve in warmed soup bowls with the Parmesan.

Cheese & Bacon Soup

serves 4

2 tbsp butter

2 garlic cloves, chopped

1 large onion, sliced

250 g/9 oz smoked lean back bacon, chopped

2 large leeks, trimmed and sliced

2 tbsp plain flour

1 litre/1¾ pints vegetable stock

450 g/1 lb potatoes, chopped

100 ml/3½ fl oz double cream

300 g/10½ oz grated Cheddar cheese, plus extra to garnish

salt and pepper

Melt the butter in a large saucepan over a medium heat. Add the garlic and onion and cook, stirring, for 3 minutes, until slightly softened. Add the chopped bacon and leeks and cook for a further 3 minutes, stirring.

In a bowl, mix the flour with enough stock to make a smooth paste, then stir it into the pan. Cook, stirring, for 2 minutes. Pour in the remaining stock, then add the potatoes. Season with salt and pepper. Bring the soup to the boil, then lower the heat and simmer gently for 25 minutes, until the potatoes are tender and cooked through.

Stir in the cream and cook for 5 minutes, then gradually stir in the cheese until melted. Remove from the heat and ladle into warmed soup bowls. Garnish with grated Cheddar cheese and serve immediately.

Sweetcorn, Potato & Cheese Soup

serves 6

25 g/1 oz butter

2 shallots, finely chopped

225 g/8 oz potatoes, diced

4 tbsp plain flour

2 tbsp dry white wine

300 ml/10 fl oz milk

325 g/11½ oz canned sweetcorn, drained

85 g/3 oz Gruyère, Emmenthal or Cheddar cheese, grated

8–10 fresh sage leaves, chopped

425 ml/15 fl oz double cream

fresh sage sprigs, to garnish

croûtons

2–3 slices of day-old white bread

2 tbsp olive oil

To make the croûtons, cut the crusts off the bread slices, then cut the remaining bread into 5-mm/¼-inch squares. Heat the olive oil in a heavy-based frying pan and add the bread cubes. Cook, tossing and stirring constantly, until evenly coloured. Drain the croûtons thoroughly on kitchen paper and reserve.

Melt the butter in a large, heavy-based saucepan. Add the shallots and cook over a low heat, stirring occasionally, for 5 minutes, or until softened. Add the potatoes and cook, stirring, for 2 minutes.

Sprinkle in the flour and cook, stirring, for 1 minute. Remove the saucepan from the heat and stir in the white wine, then gradually stir in the milk. Return the saucepan to the heat and bring to the boil, stirring constantly, then reduce the heat and simmer.

Stir in the sweetcorn kernels, grated cheese, chopped sage and cream and heat through gently until the cheese has just melted.

Ladle the soup into warmed soup bowls, scatter over the croûtons, garnish with fresh sage sprigs and serve immediately.

Minted Pea & Yogurt Soup

serves 6

2 tbsp vegetable or
sunflower oil

2 onions, coarsely chopped

225 g/8 oz potato, coarsely
chopped

2 garlic cloves, crushed

2.5-cm/1-inch piece fresh
ginger, chopped

1 tsp ground coriander

1 tsp ground cumin

1 tbsp plain flour

850 ml/1½ pints vegetable
stock

500 g/1 lb 2 oz frozen peas

2–3 tbsp chopped fresh
mint, plus extra sprigs to
garnish

150 ml/¼ pint strained
Greek yogurt, plus extra
to serve

½ tsp cornflour

300 ml/10 fl oz milk

salt and pepper

Heat the oil in a saucepan, add the onions and potato
and cook over a low heat, stirring occasionally, for about
3 minutes, until the onion is soft and translucent.

Stir in the garlic, ginger, coriander, cumin and flour and cook,
stirring constantly, for 1 minute.

Add the stock, peas and chopped mint and bring to the
boil, stirring. Reduce the heat, cover and simmer gently for
15 minutes, or until the vegetables are tender.

Process the soup, in batches, in a food processor or blender.
Return the mixture to the pan and season with salt and pepper
to taste. Blend the yogurt with the cornflour to a smooth paste
and stir into the soup. Add the milk and bring almost to the
boil, stirring constantly. Cook very gently for 2 minutes.

Serve the soup in warmed soup bowls, garnished with the mint
sprigs and a swirl of yogurt.

Clam & Sweetcorn Chowder

serves 4

750 g/1 lb 10 oz clams, or
280 g/10 oz canned clams

2 tbsp dry white wine
(if using fresh clams)

4 tsp butter

1 large onion, finely
chopped

1 small carrot, finely diced

3 tbsp plain flour

300 ml/10 fl oz fish stock

200 ml/7 fl oz water
(if using canned clams)

450 g/1 lb potatoes, diced

125 g/4 oz sweetcorn,
thawed if frozen

450 ml/16 fl oz milk

salt and pepper

chopped fresh parsley,
to garnish

If using fresh clams, wash under cold running water. Discard any with broken shells and any that refuse to close when tapped. Put the clams into a heavy-based saucepan with the wine. Cover tightly, set over a medium–high heat and cook for 2–4 minutes, or until they open, shaking the pan occasionally. Discard any that remain closed. Remove the clams from their shells and strain the cooking liquid through a very fine-meshed sieve; reserve both. If using canned clams, drain and rinse well.

Melt the butter in a large saucepan over a medium–high heat. Add the onion and carrot and cook for 3–4 minutes, stirring frequently, until the onion is softened. Stir in the flour and continue cooking for 2 minutes.

Slowly add about half the stock and stir well, scraping the bottom of the pan to mix in the flour. Pour in the remaining stock and the reserved clam cooking liquid, or the water if using canned clams, and bring just to the boil, stirring.

Add the potatoes, sweetcorn and milk and stir to combine. Reduce the heat and simmer gently, partially covered, for about 20 minutes, stirring occasionally, until all the vegetables are tender.

Chop the clams, if large. Stir in the clams and continue cooking for about 5 minutes until heated through. Taste and adjust the seasoning, if needed.

Ladle the soup into warmed soup bowls and sprinkle with parsley.

Potato & Mushroom Soup

serves 4

2 tbsp vegetable oil

600 g/1 lb 5 oz floury potatoes, sliced

1 onion, sliced

2 garlic cloves, crushed

1 litre/1¾ pints beef stock

25 g/1 oz dried mushrooms, plus extra, soaked and drained, to garnish

2 celery sticks, sliced

2 tbsp brandy

salt and pepper

topping

3 tbsp butter

2 thick slices white bread, crusts removed

55 g/2 oz Parmesan cheese, grated

chopped fresh flat-leaf parsley, to garnish

Heat the vegetable oil in a large frying pan and add the potatoes, onion and garlic. Sauté gently for 5 minutes, stirring constantly.

Add the beef stock, dried mushrooms and their strained soaking water and the celery. Bring to the boil, then reduce the heat to a simmer, cover the saucepan and cook the soup for 20 minutes, until the potatoes are tender.

Meanwhile, melt the butter for the topping in the frying pan. Sprinkle the bread slices with the grated cheese and fry the slices in the butter for 1 minute on each side, until crisp. Using a sharp knife, cut each slice into triangles.

Stir the brandy into the soup, and season to taste. Pour into warmed soup bowls and top with the fried bread triangles. Serve garnished with mushrooms and parsley.

Potato & Chickpea Soup

serves 4

1 tbsp olive oil

1 large onion, finely chopped

2–3 garlic cloves, finely chopped or crushed

1 carrot, quartered and thinly sliced

350 g/12 oz potatoes, diced

¼ tsp ground turmeric

¼ tsp garam masala

¼ tsp mild curry powder

400 g/14 oz canned chopped tomatoes

850 ml/1½ pints water

¼ tsp chilli purée, or to taste

400 g/14 oz canned chickpeas, drained and rinsed

85 g/3 oz fresh or frozen peas

salt and pepper

chopped fresh coriander, to garnish

Heat the olive oil in a large saucepan over a medium heat. Add the onion and garlic and cook, stirring occasionally, for 3–4 minutes, until the onion is beginning to soften.

Add the carrot, potatoes, turmeric, garam masala and curry powder and continue cooking for 1–2 minutes.

Add the tomatoes, measured water and chilli purée with a large pinch of salt. Reduce the heat, cover and simmer for 30 minutes, stirring occasionally.

Add the chickpeas and peas to the pan, then continue cooking for about 15 minutes, or until all the vegetables are tender.

Taste the soup and adjust the seasoning, if necessary, adding a little more chilli purée if you like. Ladle into warmed soup bowls, sprinkle with chopped coriander and serve immediately.

Chicken & Vegetable Soup

serves 4

1 litre/1¾ pints chicken stock

175 g/6 oz skinless, boneless chicken breast

fresh parsley and tarragon sprigs

2 garlic cloves, crushed

125 g/4½ oz baby carrots, halved or quartered

225 g/8 oz small new potatoes, quartered

4 tbsp plain flour

125 ml/4 fl oz milk

4–5 spring onions, sliced diagonally

85 g/3 oz asparagus tips, halved and cut into 4-cm/1½-inch pieces

125 ml/4 fl oz whipping or double cream

1 tbsp finely chopped fresh parsley

1 tbsp finely chopped fresh tarragon

salt and pepper

Put the stock in a saucepan with the chicken, parsley and tarragon sprigs and garlic. Bring just to the boil, reduce the heat, cover and simmer for 20 minutes, or until the chicken is cooked through and firm to the touch.

Remove the chicken and strain the stock. When the chicken is cool enough to handle, cut into bite-sized pieces.

Return the stock to the saucepan and bring to the boil. Adjust the heat so the liquid boils very gently. Add the carrots, cover and cook for 5 minutes. Add the potatoes, cover again and cook for about 12 minutes, or until the vegetables are beginning to soften.

Meanwhile, put the flour in a small mixing bowl and very gradually whisk in the milk to make a thick paste. Pour in a little of the hot stock mixture and stir well to make a smooth liquid.

Stir the flour mixture into the soup and bring just to the boil, stirring. Boil gently for 4–5 minutes, until it thickens, stirring frequently.

Add the spring onions, asparagus and chicken. Reduce the heat and simmer for about 15 minutes, until all the vegetables are tender. Stir in the cream and chopped herbs. Season and serve.

Spinach & Ginger Soup

serves 4

2 tbsp sunflower oil

1 onion, chopped

2 garlic cloves, finely chopped

2 tsp finely chopped fresh ginger

250 g/9 oz fresh young spinach leaves

1 small lemon grass stalk, finely chopped

1 litre/1¾ pints chicken or vegetable stock

225 g/8 oz potatoes, chopped

1 tbsp rice wine or dry sherry

1 tsp sesame oil

salt and pepper

Heat the oil in a large saucepan. Add the onion, garlic and ginger, and fry gently for 3–4 minutes, until softened but not browned.

Reserve 2–3 small spinach leaves. Add the remaining leaves and lemon grass to the saucepan, stirring until the spinach is wilted. Add the stock and potatoes to the pan and bring to the boil. Lower the heat, cover and simmer for about 10 minutes.

Tip the soup into a blender or food processor and process until completely smooth.

Return the soup to the pan and add the rice wine or sherry, then adjust the seasoning. Heat to just below boiling point.

Drizzle with a few drops of sesame oil and serve the soup hot, garnished with the reserved spinach leaves.

Potato & Split Pea Soup

serves 4

2 tbsp vegetable oil

450 g/1 lb unpeeled floury
potatoes, diced

2 onions, diced

75 g/2¾ oz split green peas

1 litre/1¾ pints vegetable
stock

60 g/2¼ oz Gruyère cheese,
grated

salt and pepper

croûtons

3 tbsp butter

1 garlic clove, crushed

1 tbsp chopped fresh
parsley

1 thick slice white bread,
diced

Heat the vegetable oil in a large saucepan. Add the potatoes and onions and sauté over a low heat, stirring constantly, for about 5 minutes.

Add the split green peas to the pan and stir together well.

Pour the vegetable stock into the pan and bring to the boil. Reduce the heat to low and simmer for about 35 minutes, until the potatoes are tender and the split peas are cooked.

Meanwhile, make the croûtons. Melt the butter in a frying pan. Add the garlic, parsley and bread cubes and cook, turning frequently, for about 2 minutes, until golden all over.

Stir the grated cheese into the soup and season to taste with salt and pepper. Heat gently until the cheese is starting to melt.

Pour the soup into warmed soup bowls and sprinkle the croûtons on top. Serve immediately.

Chicken & Potato Soup with Bacon

serves 4

1 tbsp butter

2 garlic cloves, chopped

1 onion, sliced

250 g/9 oz smoked lean back bacon, chopped

2 large leeks, sliced

2 tbsp plain flour

1 litre/1¾ pints chicken stock

800 g/1 lb 12 oz potatoes, chopped

200 g/7 oz skinless chicken breast, chopped

4 tbsp double cream

salt and pepper

grilled bacon and sprigs of fresh flat-leaf parsley, to garnish

Melt the butter in a large saucepan over a medium heat. Add the garlic and onion and cook, stirring, for 3 minutes, until slightly softened. Add the chopped bacon and leeks and cook for a further 3 minutes, stirring.

In a bowl, mix the flour with enough stock to make a smooth paste, then stir it into the pan. Cook, stirring, for 2 minutes. Pour in the remaining stock, then add the potatoes and chicken. Season with salt and pepper. Bring to the boil, then lower the heat and simmer for 25 minutes, until the chicken and potatoes are tender and cooked through.

Stir in the cream and cook for a further 2 minutes, then remove from the heat and ladle into warmed soup bowls. Garnish with the grilled bacon and flat-leaf parsley, and serve immediately.

Smoked Haddock Soup

serves 4

1 tbsp vegetable oil

55 g/2 oz smoked streaky bacon, cut into matchsticks

1 large onion, finely chopped

2 tbsp plain flour

1 litre/1¾ pints milk

700 g/1 lb 9 oz potatoes, diced

175 g/6 oz skinless smoked haddock fillet

salt and pepper

finely chopped fresh parsley, to garnish

Heat the oil in a large saucepan over a medium heat. Add the bacon and cook for 2 minutes. Stir in the onion and continue cooking for 5–7 minutes, stirring frequently, until the onion is soft and the bacon golden. Tip the pan and spoon off as much fat as possible.

Stir in the flour and continue cooking for 2 minutes. Add half of the milk and stir well, scraping the bottom of the pan to mix in the flour.

Add the potatoes and remaining milk and season with pepper. Bring just to the boil, stirring frequently, then reduce the heat and simmer gently, partially covered, for 10 minutes.

Add the fish and continue cooking, stirring occasionally, for about 15 minutes, or until the potatoes are tender and the fish breaks up easily.

Taste the soup and adjust the seasoning if necessary (salt may not be needed). Ladle into warmed soup bowls and sprinkle with chopped parsley.

Snacks &
Light Meals

Stuffed Baked Potatoes

serves 4

900 g/2 lb baking potatoes, scrubbed

2 tbsp vegetable oil

1 tsp coarse sea salt

115 g/4 oz butter

1 small onion, chopped

115 g/4 oz grated Cheddar cheese or crumbled blue cheese

salt and pepper

snipped fresh chives, to garnish

filling suggestions

4 tbsp canned, drained sweetcorn kernels

4 tbsp cooked mushrooms, courgettes or peppers

Preheat the oven to 190°C/375°F/Gas Mark 5. Prick the potatoes in several places with a fork and put on a baking tray. Brush with the oil and sprinkle with the salt. Bake in the preheated oven for 1 hour, or until the skins are crispy and the insides are soft when pierced with a fork.

Meanwhile, melt 1 tablespoon of the butter in a small frying pan over a medium–low heat. Add the onion and cook, stirring occasionally, for 8–10 minutes until soft and golden. Set aside.

Cut the potatoes in half lengthways. Scoop the flesh into a large bowl, leaving the skins intact. Reserve the skins. Increase the oven temperature to 200°C/400°F/Gas Mark 6.

Roughly mash the potato flesh and mix in the onion and remaining butter. Add salt and pepper to taste and stir in any of the filling suggestions, if using. Spoon the mixture back into the reserved potato skins. Top with the cheese.

Cook the filled potato skins in the oven for 10 minutes, or until the cheese has melted and is beginning to brown. Garnish with chives and serve at once.

Potato Fritters

serves 8

55 g/2 oz wholemeal flour

½ tsp ground coriander

½ tsp cumin seeds

¼ tsp chilli powder

½ tsp turmeric

¼ tsp salt

1 egg

3 tbsp milk

350 g/12 oz potatoes, peeled

1–2 garlic cloves, crushed

4 spring onions, chopped

55 g/2 oz sweetcorn kernels

vegetable oil, for shallow frying

Place the flour in a bowl, stir in the spices and salt and make a well in the centre. Add the egg and milk and mix to form a fairly thick batter.

Coarsely grate the potatoes, place them in a sieve and rinse well under cold running water. Drain and squeeze dry, then stir them into the batter with the garlic, spring onions and sweetcorn and mix to combine thoroughly.

Heat about 5 mm/¼ inch of vegetable oil in a large frying pan and add a few separate tablespoons of the mixture at a time, flattening each one to form a thin cake. Fry over a low heat, turning frequently, for 2–3 minutes, or until golden brown and cooked through.

Drain the fritters on absorbent kitchen paper and keep them hot while frying the remaining mixture in the same way.

Tomato & Potato Tortilla

serves 6

1 kg/2 lb 4 oz potatoes, peeled and cut into small cubes

2 tbsp olive oil

1 bunch spring onions, chopped

115 g/4 oz cherry tomatoes

6 eggs

3 tbsp water

2 tbsp chopped fresh parsley

salt and pepper

Cook the potatoes in a saucepan of lightly salted boiling water for 8–10 minutes, or until tender. Drain and reserve until required.

Preheat the grill to medium. Heat the oil in a large frying pan. Add the spring onions and fry until just soft. Add the potatoes and fry for 3–4 minutes, until coated with oil and hot. Smooth the top and scatter over the tomatoes.

Mix the eggs, water, parsley and salt and pepper together in a bowl, then pour into the frying pan. Cook over a very gentle heat for 10–15 minutes, until the tortilla looks fairly set.

Place the frying pan under the hot grill and cook until the top is brown and set. Leave to cool for 10–15 minutes before sliding out of the frying pan on to a chopping board. Cut into wedges and serve immediately.

Spanish Tortilla

serves 4–6

125 ml/4 fl oz olive oil

600 g/1 lb 5 oz potatoes, peeled and thinly sliced

1 large onion, thinly sliced

6 large eggs

salt and pepper

fresh flat-leaf parsley sprigs, to garnish

Heat a 25-cm/10-inch frying pan, preferably non-stick, over a high heat. Reduce the heat to medium–low, then add the potatoes and onion and cook, stirring occasionally, for 15–20 minutes until the potatoes are tender.

Beat the eggs in a large bowl and season generously with salt and pepper. Very gently stir the vegetables into the eggs. Set aside for 10 minutes. Drain the potatoes and onion through a sieve over a heatproof bowl to reserve the oil.

Use a wooden spoon or spatula to remove any crusty bits stuck to the base of the frying pan. Reheat the frying pan over a medium–high heat with 4 tablespoons of the reserved oil. Add the egg mixture and smooth the surface, pressing the potatoes and onions into an even layer.

Cook, shaking the pan occasionally, for 5 minutes, or until the bottom is set. Use a spatula to loosen the side of the tortilla. Put a large plate over the top and carefully invert the frying pan and plate together so that the tortilla drops onto the plate. Add 1 tablespoon of the remaining reserved oil to the frying pan and swirl around. Carefully slide the tortilla back into the pan, cooked-side up. Run the spatula around the tortilla, to tuck in the edge.

Cook for a further 3 minutes, or until the eggs are set and the bottom is golden brown. Remove from the heat and slide the tortilla onto a plate. Leave to stand for at least 5 minutes before cutting. Serve warm or at room temperature, garnished with parsley sprigs.

Onion Rösti

serves 4

450 g/1 lb floury potatoes
1 medium onion, grated
salt and pepper
oil, for shallow frying

Wash the potatoes, but do not peel them. Place in a large saucepan, cover with water and bring to the boil, covered, over a high heat. Reduce the heat and simmer for about 10 minutes, until the potatoes are just beginning to soften. Be careful not to overcook.

Drain the potatoes. Leave to cool, then peel them and grate coarsely. Mix the grated onion with the potatoes. Season the mixture with salt and pepper.

Heat the oil in a heavy-based frying pan and spoon in the potato mixture. The rösti can be as thick or as thin as you like, and can be made into one large cake or several individual ones.

Cook over a high heat for about 5 minutes, until the bottom is golden, then turn and cook until the second side is brown and crispy. Remove from the heat, drain and serve.

Potato, Fontina & Rosemary Tart

serves 4

1 quantity puff pastry

plain flour, for dusting

filling

3–4 waxy potatoes

300 g/10½ oz fontina cheese, cut into cubes

1 red onion, thinly sliced

3 large fresh rosemary sprigs

2 tbsp olive oil

1 egg yolk

salt and pepper

Preheat the oven to 190°C/375°F/Gas Mark 5. Roll out the pastry on a lightly floured work surface into a round about 25 cm/10 inches in diameter and put on a baking tray.

Peel the potatoes and slice as thinly as possible so that they are almost transparent – use a mandolin if you have one. Arrange the potato slices in a spiral, overlapping the slices to cover the pastry but leaving a 2-cm/¾-inch margin around the edge.

Arrange the cheese and onion over the potatoes, scatter with the rosemary and drizzle over the oil. Season to taste with salt and pepper and brush the edges with the egg yolk to glaze.

Bake in the preheated oven for 25 minutes, or until the potatoes are tender and the pastry is brown and crisp.

Potato Skins with Tomato & Sweetcorn Salsa

serves 4

2 large baking potatoes

tomato & sweetcorn salsa

85 g/3 oz canned sweetcorn kernels

55 g/2 oz canned kidney beans

2 tbsp olive oil, plus extra for brushing

115 g/4 oz tomatoes, deseeded and diced

2 shallots, finely sliced

¼ red pepper, finely diced

1 fresh red chilli, deseeded and finely chopped

1 tbsp chopped fresh coriander leaves

1 tbsp lime juice

55 g/2 oz Cheddar cheese, grated

salt and pepper

Preheat the oven to 200°C/400°F/Gas Mark 6. Prick the potatoes in several places with a fork and brush with oil. Cook directly on the oven shelf for 1 hour, or until the skins are crispy and the insides are soft when pierced with a fork.

Meanwhile, make the salsa. Drain the sweetcorn and beans, rinse well, then drain again. Put in a bowl with the oil, tomatoes, shallots, red pepper, chilli, coriander, lime juice and salt and pepper to taste and mix well together.

Preheat the grill to medium. Cut the potatoes in half lengthways. Scoop out the flesh (reserve for use in another recipe), leaving the skins intact. Brush the insides with oil, then put on a baking tray, cut-sides up. Cook under the grill for 5 minutes, or until crisp.

Spoon the salsa into the potato skins and sprinkle the cheese over the top. Return the filled potato skins to the grill and cook gently until the cheese has melted. Serve immediately.

Potato, Beef & Leek Pasties

makes 4

butter, for greasing

225 g/8 oz waxy potatoes, diced

1 small carrot, diced

225 g/8 oz beef steak, cubed

1 leek, sliced

225 g/8 oz ready-made shortcrust pastry

plain flour, for dusting

15 g/½ oz butter

1 egg, beaten

salt and pepper

Preheat the oven to 200°C/400°F/Gas Mark 6. Lightly grease a baking sheet with butter. Mix the potatoes, carrot, beef and leek together in a large bowl. Season well with salt and pepper.

Divide the shortcrust pastry into 4 equal portions. Roll each portion out on a lightly floured work surface into a 20-cm/8-inch round.

Spoon the potato mixture onto one half of each round, to within 1 cm/½ inch of the edge. Top the potato mixture with the butter, dividing it equally between the rounds. Brush the pastry edge with a little of the beaten egg.

Fold the pastry over to encase the filling and crimp the edges together. Transfer the pasties to the prepared baking sheet and brush them with the beaten egg.

Cook the pasties in the preheated oven for 20 minutes. Reduce the oven temperature to 160°C/325°F/Gas Mark 3 and cook the pasties for a further 30 minutes until cooked through.

Vegetable Samosas

makes 12

filling

2 tbsp vegetable oil

1 onion, chopped

½ tsp ground coriander

½ tsp ground cumin

pinch of ground turmeric

½ tsp ground ginger

½ tsp garam masala

1 garlic clove, crushed

225 g/8 oz potatoes, diced

100 g/3½ oz frozen peas, thawed

150 g/5½ oz spinach, chopped

pastry

350 g/12 oz (12 sheets) filo pastry

oil, for deep-frying

To make the filling, heat the oil in a frying pan. Add the onion and sauté, stirring frequently, for 1–2 minutes, until softened. Stir in all of the spices and garlic and cook for 1 minute.

Add the potatoes and cook over a low heat, stirring frequently, for 5 minutes, until they begin to soften.

Stir in the peas and spinach and cook for a further 3–4 minutes.

Lay the filo pastry sheets out on a clean work surface and fold each sheet in half lengthways.

Place 2 tablespoons of the vegetable filling at one end of each folded pastry sheet. Fold over one corner to make a triangle. Continue folding in this way to make a triangular package and seal the edges with water.

Repeat with the remaining pastry and the remaining filling.

Heat the oil for deep-frying to 180°C/350°F or until a cube of bread browns in 30 seconds. Fry the samosas, in batches, for 1–2 minutes, until golden. Drain on absorbent kitchen paper and keep warm while cooking the remainder. Serve immediately.

Potato & Cauliflower Fritters

serves 4

225 g/8 oz floury potatoes, diced

225 g/8 oz cauliflower florets

35 g/1¼ oz Parmesan cheese, grated

1 egg, plus 1 egg white

oil, for frying

paprika, for dusting (optional)

salt and pepper

crispy bacon slices, chopped, to serve

Cook the potatoes in a saucepan of boiling water for 10 minutes, until cooked through. Drain well and mash until smooth.

Meanwhile, cook the cauliflower florets in a separate pan of boiling water for 10 minutes.

Drain the cauliflower florets and then add them to the mashed potato. Gently stir in the grated Parmesan cheese and season to taste with salt and pepper.

Separate the whole egg and beat the yolk into the potato and cauliflower, mixing well.

Lightly whisk both the egg whites in a clean bowl, then carefully fold into the potato and cauliflower mixture.

Divide the potato mixture into 8 equal portions and then shape them into rounds.

Heat the oil in a frying pan and cook the fritters for 3–5 minutes, turning once halfway through cooking. Dust the cooked fritters with a little paprika, if desired, and then serve them at once accompanied by the crispy chopped bacon.

Sweet Potato Cakes with Soy-tomato Sauce

serves 4

500 g/1 lb 2 oz sweet
potatoes

2 garlic cloves, crushed

1 small fresh green chilli,
deseeded and chopped

2 fresh coriander sprigs,
chopped

1 tbsp dark soy sauce

plain flour, for shaping

vegetable oil, for frying

sesame seeds,
for sprinkling

soy-tomato sauce

2 tsp vegetable oil

1 garlic clove, finely
chopped

1½ tsp finely chopped
fresh ginger

3 tomatoes, skinned and
chopped

2 tbsp dark soy sauce

1 tbsp lime juice

2 tbsp chopped fresh
coriander

To make the soy-tomato sauce, heat the oil in a wok and stir-fry the garlic and ginger over a medium heat for about 1 minute. Add the tomatoes and stir-fry for a further 2 minutes. Remove the wok from the heat and stir in the soy sauce, lime juice and chopped coriander. Reserve and keep warm.

Peel the sweet potatoes and grate finely (you can do this quickly with a food processor). Place the garlic, chilli and coriander in a mortar and crush to a smooth paste with a pestle. Stir in the soy sauce and mix with the sweet potatoes.

Put some flour on a plate. Divide the mixture into 12 equal portions, toss each portion in the flour until coated and pat into a flat, round patty shape.

Heat a shallow layer of oil in a wide frying pan. Fry the sweet potato patties, in batches, over a high heat until golden, turning once.

Drain the sweet potato cakes on kitchen paper, transfer to a warm serving dish, sprinkle with sesame seeds and serve hot, with the soy-tomato sauce.

Mixed Mushroom Cakes

serves 4

500 g/1 lb 2 oz floury
potatoes, diced

2 tbsp butter

175 g/6 oz mixed
mushrooms, chopped

2 garlic cloves, crushed

1 small egg, beaten

1 tbsp snipped fresh chives,
plus extra to garnish

plain flour, for coating

vegetable oil, for frying

salt and pepper

salad, to serve

Cook the potatoes in a pan of lightly salted, boiling water for 10 minutes, or until cooked through.

Drain the potatoes well, mash with a potato masher or fork and reserve.

Meanwhile, melt the butter in a frying pan. Add the mushrooms and garlic and cook, stirring constantly, for 5 minutes. Drain well.

Stir the mushrooms and garlic into the potatoes, together with the beaten egg and chives.

Put some flour on a plate. Divide the mixture into four equal portions and shape them into round cakes with your hands. Toss them in the flour until the outsides of the cakes are completely coated, shaking off any excess.

Heat the oil in a frying pan. Add the potato cakes and fry over a medium heat for 10 minutes, until they are golden brown, turning them over halfway through. Serve the cakes at once, with a simple crisp salad.

Salmon Pancakes

serves 4

450 g/1 lb floury potatoes, grated

2 spring onions, chopped

2 tbsp self-raising flour

2 eggs, beaten

2 tbsp vegetable oil

salt and pepper

fresh chives, to garnish

topping

150 ml/5 fl oz soured cream

125 g/4½ oz smoked salmon

Rinse the grated potatoes under cold running water, drain and pat dry on kitchen paper. Transfer to a mixing bowl.

Mix the spring onions, flour and eggs into the potatoes and season well with salt and pepper.

Heat 1 tablespoon of the oil in a frying pan. Drop about four separate tablespoons of the mixture into the pan and spread each one with the back of a spoon to form a round (the mixture should make 16 pancakes). Cook for 5–7 minutes, turning once, until golden. Drain well.

Heat the remaining oil and cook the remaining mixture in batches.

Top the pancakes with the soured cream and smoked salmon, garnish with fresh chives and serve hot.

Fish Cakes

serves 4

450 g/1 lb potatoes, peeled

450 g/1 lb mixed fish fillets,
such as cod, haddock
and salmon, skinned

2 tbsp chopped fresh
parsley or tarragon

grated zest of 1 lemon

1 tbsp plain flour

1 egg, beaten

115 g/4 oz white or
wholemeal breadcrumbs,
made from day-old bread

4 tbsp vegetable oil,
for frying

salt and pepper

Cut the potatoes into chunks and cook in a large saucepan of boiling, salted water for 15 minutes. Drain well and mash with a potato masher until smooth.

Place the fish in a frying pan and just cover with water. Bring to the boil over a medium heat, then cover and simmer gently for 5 minutes until just cooked. Remove from the heat and drain the fish onto a plate. When cool enough to handle, flake the fish and ensure that no bones remain.

Mix the potatoes with the fish, herbs and lemon zest in a bowl. Season well and shape into four round, flat cakes.

Dust the cakes with flour, dip them into the beaten egg, then coat thoroughly in the breadcrumbs. Place on a baking sheet, cover with clingfilm and allow to chill for at least half an hour.

Heat the oil in the frying pan and fry the cakes over medium heat for 5 minutes on each side. Use a palette knife or fish slice to turn them carefully. Serve.

Feisty Potatoes

serves 6

chilli oil

150 ml/5 fl oz olive oil

2 small fresh red chillies, split

1 tsp hot Spanish paprika

potatoes

2 tbsp olive oil

1 kg/2 lb 4 oz potatoes, unpeeled, cut into chunks

mayonnaise, to serve

To make the chilli oil, heat the oil and chillies in a heavy-based frying pan over a high heat until the chillies begin to sizzle. Remove from the heat and stir in the paprika. Set aside and leave to cool, then transfer the oil to a pourer with a spout. Do not strain.

Heat the olive oil in a large, heavy-based frying pan over a medium heat, add the potatoes and cook, stirring occasionally, for 15 minutes until golden brown all over and tender. Remove with a slotted spoon and transfer to a plate covered in kitchen paper. Blot off the excess oil.

To serve, divide the potatoes between 6 serving plates and add a dollop of mayonnaise to each. Drizzle with the chilli oil and serve warm or at room temperature.

Raita Potatoes

serves 4–8

400 g/14 oz new potatoes, scrubbed

1 tsp coriander seeds

1 tsp fennel seeds

400 ml/14 fl oz natural yogurt

1 fresh green chilli, deseeded and finely chopped

salt and pepper

chopped fresh mint, to garnish

4–8 poppadoms, warmed, to serve

Boil the potatoes in salted water for 10–12 minutes, or until tender when pierced with a fork. Drain and rinse with cold water to cool, then shake dry. When cool enough to handle, finely chop the potatoes, with or without peeling them.

Meanwhile, dry-fry the coriander and fennel seeds in a hot frying pan over a high heat, stirring them around constantly, until you can smell the aromas. Immediately tip the spices out of the pan so they do not burn.

Put the spices in a spice grinder or use a pestle and mortar to grind to a fine powder. Beat the yogurt in a bowl until it is smooth, then stir in the ground spices, chilli and salt and pepper to taste. Add the potato chunks and stir together without breaking up the potatoes. Cover the bowl with clingfilm and chill for at least 30 minutes.

When ready to serve, give the potatoes and yogurt a quick stir, then add lots of chopped fresh mint. Serve with warmed poppadoms.

Creamy Stuffed Mushrooms

serves 4

25 g/1 oz dried ceps

225 g/8 oz floury potatoes, diced

2 tbsp butter, melted

4 tbsp double cream

2 tbsp snipped fresh chives

8 large open-capped mushrooms

25 g/1 oz Emmenthal cheese, grated

150 ml/5 fl oz vegetable stock

salt and pepper

Place the dried ceps in a small bowl. Add sufficient boiling water to cover and leave to soak for 20 minutes.

Meanwhile, cook the potatoes in a medium saucepan of lightly salted, boiling water for 10 minutes, until cooked through and tender. Drain well and mash until smooth.

Drain the soaked ceps and then chop them finely. Mix them into the mashed potato.

Thoroughly blend the butter, cream and snipped chives together and pour the mixture into the ceps and potato mixture, mixing well. Season to taste with salt and pepper.

Remove the stalks from the open-capped mushrooms. Chop the stalks and stir them into the potato mixture. Spoon the mixture into the open-capped mushrooms and sprinkle the cheese over the top.

Arrange the filled mushrooms in a shallow ovenproof dish and pour in the vegetable stock.

Cover the dish and cook in a preheated oven, 220°C/425°F/Gas Mark 7, for 20 minutes. Remove the lid and cook for a further 5 minutes, until golden. Serve the mushrooms immediately.

Smoked Fish & Potato Pâté

serves 4

650 g/1 lb 7 oz floury potatoes, diced

300 g/10½ oz smoked mackerel fillets, skinned and flaked

75 g/2¾ oz cooked gooseberries

2 tsp lemon juice

2 tbsp low-fat crème fraîche

1 tbsp capers

1 gherkin, chopped

1 tbsp chopped dill pickle

1 tbsp chopped fresh dill

salt and pepper

toast or warm crusty bread, to serve

Cook the diced potatoes in a large saucepan of boiling water for 10 minutes, until tender, then drain well.

Place the cooked potatoes in a food processor or blender.

Add the skinned and flaked smoked mackerel and process for 30 seconds, until fairly smooth. Alternatively, place the ingredients in a bowl and then mash them with a fork.

Add the cooked gooseberries, lemon juice and crème fraîche to the fish and potato mixture. Blend for a further 10 seconds or mash well.

Stir in the capers, gherkin, dill pickle and fresh dill. Season well with salt and pepper.

Turn the fish pâté into a serving dish and serve with slices of toast or warm crusty bread.

Main
Dishes

Potato Ravioli

serves 6

filling

1 tbsp vegetable oil

125 g/4½ oz fresh beef mince

1 shallot, diced

1 garlic clove, crushed

1 tbsp plain flour

1 tbsp tomato purée

150 ml/5 fl oz beef stock

1 celery stick, chopped

2 tomatoes, skinned and diced

2 tsp chopped fresh basil

salt and pepper

ravioli

450 g/1 lb floury potatoes, diced

3 small egg yolks

3 tbsp olive oil

175 g/6 oz plain flour, plus extra for dusting

5 tbsp butter, for frying

salt and pepper

basil leaves, to garnish

To make the filling, heat the oil in a pan and fry the beef for 3–4 minutes, breaking it up with a spoon. Add the shallot and garlic and cook for 2–3 minutes, until the shallot has softened.

Stir in the flour and tomato purée and cook for 1 minute. Stir in the beef stock, celery, tomatoes and chopped fresh basil. Season to taste with salt and pepper.

Cook the mixture over a low heat for 20 minutes. Remove from the heat and leave to cool.

To make the ravioli, cook the potatoes in a pan of boiling water for 10 minutes, until tender.

Mash the potatoes and place them in a mixing bowl. Blend in the egg yolks and oil. Season with salt and pepper, then stir in the flour and mix to form a dough.

On a lightly floured surface, divide the dough into 24 pieces and shape into flat rounds. Spoon the filling onto one half of each round and fold the dough over to encase the filling, pressing down firmly to seal the edges.

Melt the butter in a frying pan and cook the ravioli in batches for 6–8 minutes, turning once, until golden. Serve hot, garnished with fresh basil leaves.

Potato Gnocchi with Walnut Pesto

serves 4

450 g/1 lb floury potatoes

55 g/2 oz Parmesan cheese, grated

1 egg, beaten

200 g/7 oz plain flour, plus extra for dusting

walnut pesto

40 g/1½ oz fresh flat-leaf parsley

2 tbsp capers, rinsed

2 garlic cloves

175 ml/6 fl oz extra virgin olive oil

70 g/2½ oz walnut halves

40 g/1½ oz shavings of fresh Parmesan

salt and pepper

Boil the potatoes in their skins in a large saucepan of water for 30–35 minutes until tender. Drain well and leave to cool slightly.

Meanwhile, to make the Walnut Pesto, chop the parsley, capers and garlic, then put in a mortar with the oil, walnuts, and salt and pepper to taste. Pound to a coarse paste in a mortar with a pestle. Add the Parmesan cheese and stir well.

When the potatoes are cool enough to handle, peel off the skins and pass the flesh through a sieve into a large bowl or press through a potato ricer. While still hot, season well with salt and pepper and add the Parmesan cheese. Beat in the egg and sift in the flour. Lightly mix together, then turn out on to a lightly floured work surface. Knead lightly until the mixture becomes a smooth dough. If it is too sticky, add a little more flour.

Using your hands, roll out the dough on a lightly floured work surface into a long log. Cut into 2.5-cm/1-inch pieces and gently press with a fork to give the traditional ridged effect. Transfer to a floured baking sheet and cover with a clean tea towel while you make the remaining gnocchi.

Bring a large saucepan of water to the boil, add the gnocchi, in small batches, and cook for 1–2 minutes. Remove with a slotted spoon and transfer to a warmed serving dish to keep warm while you cook the remaining gnocchi.

Serve the gnocchi in warmed serving bowls with a good spoonful of the walnut pesto on top.

Meatballs in Spicy Sauce

serves 4

225 g/8 oz floury potatoes, diced

225 g/8 oz beef or lamb mince

1 onion, finely chopped

1 tbsp chopped fresh coriander

1 celery stick, finely chopped

2 garlic cloves, crushed

2 tbsp butter

1 tbsp vegetable oil

salt and pepper

chopped fresh coriander, to garnish

sauce

1 tbsp vegetable oil

1 onion, finely chopped

2 tsp soft brown sugar

400 g/14 oz canned chopped tomatoes

1 fresh green chilli, deseeded and chopped

1 tsp paprika

150 ml/5 fl oz vegetable stock

2 tsp cornflour

Cook the diced potatoes in a saucepan of boiling water for 25 minutes, until cooked through. Drain well and transfer to a large mixing bowl. Mash until smooth.

Add the beef or lamb mince, onion, coriander, celery, garlic and seasoning and mix together well.

Bring the mixture together with your hands and roll it into 20 small balls.

To make the sauce, heat the oil in a pan and sauté the onion for 5 minutes. Add the remaining sauce ingredients and bring to the boil, stirring constantly. Lower the heat and simmer for 20 minutes.

Meanwhile, heat the butter and oil for the meatballs in a frying pan. Add the meatballs, in batches, and cook, turning frequently, for 10–15 minutes, until browned. Keep warm while cooking the remainder. Transfer the meatballs to a warm, shallow dish and serve, with the sauce poured around them, garnished with the fresh coriander.

Potato & Pepperoni Pizza

serves 4

1 tbsp butter, plus extra for greasing

plain flour, for dusting

900 g/2 lb floury potatoes, diced

1 tbsp butter

2 garlic cloves, crushed

2 tbsp chopped mixed fresh herbs

1 egg, beaten

6 tbsp passata

2 tbsp tomato purée

50 g/1¾ oz pepperoni slices

1 green pepper, deseeded and cut into strips

1 yellow pepper, deseeded and cut into strips

2 large open-capped mushrooms, sliced

25 g/1 oz stoned black olives, quartered

125 g/4½ oz mozzarella cheese, sliced

Grease and flour a 23-cm/9-inch pizza pan. Cook the potatoes in a pan of boiling water for 10 minutes, or until tender. Drain and mash, then transfer to a mixing bowl and stir in the butter, garlic, herbs and egg.

Spread the mixture into the prepared pizza pan. Cook in a preheated oven, 220°C/425°F/Gas Mark 7, for 7–10 minutes, until set.

Mix the passata and tomato purée together and spoon it over the pizza base, to within 1 cm/½ inch of the edge of the base.

Arrange the pepperoni slices and the peppers, mushrooms and olives on top of the passata.

Scatter the mozzarella cheese on top of the pizza. Return to the oven for 20 minutes, or until the base is cooked through and the cheese has melted on top. Serve hot.

Bubble & Squeak

serves 2–3

450 g/1 lb green cabbage

1 onion, thinly sliced

4 tbsp olive oil

salt and pepper

mashed potato

450 g/1 lb floury potatoes, such as King Edward

55 g/2 oz butter

3 tbsp hot milk

salt and pepper

To make the mashed potato, cook the potatoes in a large saucepan of boiling salted water for 15–20 minutes. Drain well and mash with a potato masher until smooth. Season with salt and pepper, add the butter and milk and stir well.

Cut the cabbage into quarters, remove the centre stalk and shred the leaves finely.

In a large frying pan, fry the onion in half the oil until soft. Add the cabbage to the pan and stir-fry for 2–3 minutes until softened. Season with salt and pepper, add the mashed potato and mix together well.

Press the mixture firmly into the frying pan and allow to cook over a high heat for 4–5 minutes so that the base is crispy. Place a plate over the frying pan and invert the pan so that the potato cake falls onto the plate. Add the remaining oil to the pan, reheat and slip the cake back into the pan with the uncooked side down.

Continue to cook for a further 5 minutes until the bottom is crispy too. Turn out onto a hot plate and cut into wedges for serving. Serve immediately.

Potato & Aubergine Bake

serves 4

500 g/1 lb 2 oz waxy
potatoes, sliced

1 tbsp vegetable oil

1 onion, chopped

2 garlic cloves, crushed

500 g/1 lb 2 oz firm tofu,
drained and diced

2 tbsp tomato purée

2 tbsp plain flour

300 ml/10 fl oz vegetable
stock

2 large tomatoes, sliced

1 aubergine, sliced

2 tbsp chopped fresh
thyme

450 ml/16 fl oz natural
yogurt

2 eggs, beaten

salt and pepper

Cook the sliced potatoes in a saucepan of boiling water
for 10 minutes, until tender but not breaking up. Drain
and reserve.

Heat the oil in a frying pan. Add the onion and garlic and
fry, stirring occasionally, for 2–3 minutes.

Add the tofu, tomato purée and flour and cook for
1 minute. Gradually stir in the stock and bring to the boil,
stirring. Reduce the heat and simmer for 10 minutes.

Arrange a layer of the potato slices in the base of a deep
ovenproof dish. Spoon the tofu mixture evenly on top. Layer
the sliced tomatoes, then the aubergine and finally, the
remaining potato slices on top of the tofu mixture, making
sure that it is completely covered. Sprinkle with thyme.

Mix the yogurt and beaten eggs together in a bowl and
season to taste with salt and pepper. Spoon the yogurt
topping over the sliced potatoes to cover them completely.

Bake in a preheated oven, 190°C/ 375°F/Gas Mark 5,
for about 35–45 minutes, or until the topping is browned.
Serve the gratin immediately.

Layered Fish & Potato Pie

serves 4

900 g/2 lb waxy potatoes, sliced

5 tbsp butter

1 red onion, halved and sliced

5 tbsp plain flour

450 ml/16 fl oz milk

150 ml/5 fl oz double cream

225 g/8 oz smoked haddock fillet, skinned and diced

225 g/8 oz cod fillet, skinned and diced

1 red pepper, deseeded and diced

125 g/4½ oz broccoli florets

50 g/1¾ oz Parmesan cheese, grated

salt and pepper

Cook the sliced potatoes in a saucepan of boiling water for 10 minutes. Drain and reserve.

Meanwhile, melt the butter in a saucepan, add the onion and fry gently for 3–4 minutes.

Add the flour and cook for 1 minute. Blend in the milk and cream and bring to the boil, stirring until the sauce has thickened.

Arrange about half of the potato slices in the base of a shallow, ovenproof dish.

Add the fish, red pepper and broccoli to the sauce and cook over a low heat for 10 minutes. Season with salt and pepper, then spoon the mixture over the potatoes in the dish.

Arrange the remaining potato slices in a layer over the fish mixture. Sprinkle the Parmesan cheese over the top.

Cook in a preheated oven, 180°C/350°F/Gas Mark 4, for about 30 minutes, until the top is golden.

Potato, Leek & Chicken Pie

serves 4

225 g/8 oz waxy potatoes, diced

5 tbsp butter

1 skinned chicken breast fillet, about 175 g/6 oz, diced

1 leek, sliced

150 g/5½ oz chestnut mushrooms, sliced

2½ tbsp plain flour

300 ml/10 fl oz milk

1 tbsp Dijon mustard

2 tbsp chopped fresh sage

225 g/8 oz filo pastry, thawed if frozen

3 tbsp butter, melted

salt and pepper

Cook the diced potatoes in a saucepan of boiling water for 5 minutes. Drain and reserve.

Melt the butter in a frying pan and cook the diced chicken for 5 minutes, or until browned all over.

Add the leek and mushrooms and cook over a medium heat, stirring frequently, for 3 minutes. Stir in the flour and cook for 1 minute, stirring constantly. Gradually add the milk and bring to the boil. Add the mustard, sage and potatoes, then simmer for 10 minutes.

Meanwhile, line a deep pie dish with half of the sheets of filo pastry. Spoon the sauce into the dish and cover with one sheet of pastry. Brush the pastry with melted butter and lay another sheet on top. Brush this sheet with melted butter.

Cut the remaining filo pastry into strips and fold them on to the top of the pie to create a ruffled effect. Brush the strips with the remaining melted butter and cook in a preheated oven, 180°C/350°F/Gas Mark 4, for about 45 minutes, or until golden brown and crisp. Serve hot.

Potato, Sausage & Onion Pie

serves 4

2 large waxy potatoes, unpeeled and sliced

2 tbsp butter

4 thick pork and herb sausages

1 leek, sliced

2 garlic cloves, crushed

150 ml/5 fl oz vegetable stock

150 ml/5 fl oz dry cider or apple juice

2 tbsp chopped fresh sage

2 tbsp cornflour

4 tbsp water

75 g/2¾ oz mature cheese, grated

salt and pepper

Cook the sliced potatoes in a saucepan of boiling water for 10 minutes. Drain and reserve.

Meanwhile, melt the butter in a frying pan and cook the sausages for 8–10 minutes, turning them frequently so that they brown on all sides. Remove the sausages from the pan and cut them into thick slices.

Add the leek, garlic and sausage slices to the pan and cook for 2–3 minutes.

Add the vegetable stock, cider and sage. Season with salt and pepper to taste.

Blend the cornflour with the water. Stir it into the pan and bring to the boil, stirring until the sauce is thick and clear. Spoon the mixture into the base of a deep pie dish.

Layer the potato slices on top. Season to taste with salt and pepper and sprinkle the grated cheese over the top.

Cook in a preheated oven, 190°C/375°F/Gas Mark 5, for 25–30 minutes, or until the potatoes are cooked and the cheese is golden brown. Serve hot.

Lamb & Potato Moussaka

serves 4

1 large aubergine, sliced

1 tbsp olive or vegetable oil

1 onion, finely chopped

1 garlic clove, crushed

350 g/12 oz fresh lean lamb mince

250 g/9 oz mushrooms, sliced

425 g/15 oz canned chopped tomatoes with herbs

150 ml/5 fl oz lamb or vegetable stock

2 tbsp cornflour

2 tbsp water

500 g/1 lb 2 oz potatoes, parboiled for 10 minutes and sliced

2 eggs

125 g/4½ oz low-fat soft cheese

150 ml/5 fl oz low-fat natural yogurt

55 g/2 oz grated low-fat mature Cheddar cheese

salt and pepper

Lay the aubergine slices on a clean surface and sprinkle liberally with salt, to extract the bitter juices. Leave for 10 minutes then turn the slices over and repeat. Put in a colander, rinse and drain well.

Meanwhile, heat the oil in a saucepan and fry the onion and garlic for 3–4 minutes. Add the lamb and mushrooms and cook for about 5 minutes, until browned. Stir in the tomatoes and stock, bring to the boil and simmer for 10 minutes. Mix the cornflour and water to a smooth paste and add to the pan. Cook, stirring, until thickened.

Spoon half the mixture into an ovenproof dish. Cover with the aubergine slices, then the remaining lamb mixture. Arrange the sliced potatoes on top.

Beat together the eggs, soft cheese and yogurt and season to taste with salt and pepper. Pour over the potatoes to cover them completely. Sprinkle with the grated cheese.

Bake in a preheated oven, 190°C/375°F/Gas Mark 5, for 45 minutes, until the topping is set and golden brown.

Pepper & Mushroom Hash

serves 4

675 g/1lb 8 oz potatoes,
diced

1 tbsp olive oil

2 garlic cloves, crushed

1 green pepper, deseeded
and diced

1 yellow pepper, deseeded
and diced

3 tomatoes, diced

75 g/2¾ oz button
mushrooms, halved

1 tbsp Worcestershire
sauce

2 tbsp chopped fresh basil

salt and pepper

fresh basil leaves,
to garnish

Cook the diced potatoes in a large saucepan of lightly salted, boiling water for 7–8 minutes. Drain well and reserve.

Heat the olive oil in a large, heavy-based frying pan. Add the potatoes and cook over a medium heat, stirring constantly, for about 8–10 minutes, until browned.

Add the garlic and peppers and cook, stirring frequently, for 2–3 minutes.

Stir in the tomatoes and mushrooms and cook, stirring frequently, for 5–6 minutes.

Stir in the Worcestershire sauce and basil and season to taste with salt and pepper. Transfer to a warmed serving dish and garnish with basil sprigs.

Tagine of Monkfish, Potatoes, Cherry Tomatoes & Olives

serves 4–6

about 1 kg/2 lb 4 oz monkfish tail, cut into chunks

2 green peppers

about 12 small new potatoes, peeled

3–4 tbsp olive oil, plus extra for drizzling

4–5 garlic cloves, thinly sliced

about 12 cherry tomatoes

large handful of kalamata or fleshy black olives

100 ml/3½ fl oz water

salt and pepper

chermoula

2 garlic cloves

1 tsp sea salt

2 tsp ground cumin

1 tsp paprika

juice of 1 lemon

1 small bunch fresh coriander, roughly chopped

1 tbsp olive oil

First make the chermoula. Pound the garlic and salt in a mortar with a pestle to a smooth paste. Add the cumin, paprika, lemon juice and coriander and blend with the oil. Put the monkfish in a non-metallic dish or bowl. Reserve about 1 tablespoon of the chermoula, then rub the remaining chermoula over the monkfish chunks. Cover the dish and leave to marinate in the refrigerator for 1 hour.

Meanwhile, using tongs, carefully hold the peppers directly over a gas flame for about 10 minutes, or until the skin buckles. Put the charred peppers in a polythene bag and leave to sweat for 5 minutes, then hold them by the stems under cold running water and peel off the skins. Put the peppers on a chopping board, remove the stems and seeds and cut the flesh into thick strips. Set aside. At the same time, parboil the potatoes in plenty of water for 8 minutes, or until slightly softened. Drain, refresh and halve lengthways.

Heat 2–3 tablespoons of the oil in a tagine or heavy-based, flameproof casserole, add the garlic and cook over a medium heat, stirring, for 1–2 minutes.

Gently toss the fish with the rest of the ingredients and serve.

Roast Pork with Rosemary Potatoes

serves 4

1 leg of pork, weighing
1 kg/2 lb 4 oz

1 tablespoon olive oil

salt

rosemary potatoes

1 kg/2 lb 4 oz floury
potatoes

4 tbsp olive oil

1 bunch fresh rosemary,
chopped

Preheat the oven to 220°C/425°F/Gas Mark 7.

Make sure that the skin of the pork is well scored and dry. Put into a roasting tin. Brush the skin with the oil and rub liberally with salt. Roast in the preheated oven for 20 minutes, or until the skin has started to blister and crisp. Reduce the heat to 200°C/400°F/Gas Mark 6 and roast for a further 40 minutes, or until the pork is cooked through and the skin is crisp and golden. Remove from the oven and ensure that the juices run clear when a skewer is inserted deep into the meat. Leave to rest for 20 minutes before slicing.

Meanwhile, for the rosemary potatoes, peel the potatoes and cut into medium dice. Heat the oil in a separate roasting tin in the oven. When hot, add the potatoes and rosemary, toss to coat and roast for 40 minutes, or until crisp and golden. Remove from the tin and scatter with a little salt. Serve immediately with the sliced pork.

Potato Stir Fry

serves 4

900 g/2 lb waxy potatoes

2 tbsp vegetable oil

1 yellow pepper, deseeded and diced

1 red pepper, deseeded and diced

1 carrot, cut into matchsticks

1 courgette, cut into matchsticks

2 garlic cloves, crushed

1 fresh red chilli, deseeded and sliced

1 bunch spring onions, halved lengthways

125 ml/4 fl oz coconut milk

1 tsp chopped lemon grass

2 tsp lime juice

finely grated rind of 1 lime

1 tbsp chopped fresh coriander

Using a sharp knife, cut the potatoes into small cubes.

Bring a large saucepan of water to the boil over a medium heat, add the diced potatoes and cook for 5 minutes. Drain thoroughly.

Heat a wok or large, heavy-based frying pan, add the vegetable oil and heat, swirling the oil around the base of the wok or pan until it is really hot.

Add the potatoes, yellow and red peppers, carrot, courgette, garlic and chilli to the wok or pan and stir-fry over a medium heat for 2–3 minutes.

Stir in the spring onions, coconut milk, lemon grass and lime juice and stir-fry the mixture for a further 5 minutes.

Add the lime rind and chopped fresh coriander and stir-fry for 1 minute. Serve immediately while hot.

Chicken & Barley Stew

serves 4

2 tbsp vegetable oil

8 small, skinless chicken thighs

500 ml/18 fl oz chicken stock

100 g/3½ oz pearl barley, rinsed and drained

200 g/7 oz small new potatoes, scrubbed and halved lengthways

2 large carrots, peeled and sliced

1 leek, trimmed and sliced

2 shallots, sliced

1 tbsp tomato purée

1 bay leaf

1 courgette, trimmed and sliced

2 tbsp chopped fresh flat-leaf parsley, plus extra sprigs to garnish

2 tbsp plain flour

4 tablespoons water

salt and pepper

Heat the oil in a large pot over a medium heat. Add the chicken and cook for 3 minutes, then turn over and cook on the other side for a further 2 minutes. Add the stock, barley, potatoes, carrots, leek, shallots, tomato purée and bay leaf. Bring to the boil, lower the heat and simmer for 30 minutes.

Add the courgette and chopped parsley, cover the pan and cook for a further 20 minutes, or until the chicken is cooked through. Remove the bay leaf and discard.

In a separate bowl, mix the flour with the water and stir into a smooth paste. Add it to the stew and cook, stirring, over a low heat for a further 5 minutes. Season to taste with salt and pepper.

Remove from the heat, ladle into individual serving bowls and garnish with sprigs of fresh parsley.

Irish Stew

serves 4

4 tbsp plain flour

1.3 kg/3 lb middle neck of lamb, trimmed of visible fat

3 large onions, chopped

3 carrots, sliced

450 g/1 lb potatoes, quartered

½ tsp dried thyme

850 ml/1½ pints hot beef stock

salt and pepper

2 tbsp chopped fresh parsley, to garnish

Preheat the oven to 160°C/325°F/Gas Mark 3. Spread the flour on a plate and season with salt and pepper. Roll the pieces of lamb in the flour to coat, shaking off any excess, and arrange in the base of a casserole.

Layer the onions, carrots and potatoes on top of the lamb.

Sprinkle in the thyme and pour in the stock, then cover and cook in the preheated oven for 2½ hours. Garnish with the chopped fresh parsley and serve straight from the casserole.

Mixed Vegetable Curry

serves 4

1 aubergine

225 g/8 oz turnips

350 g/12 oz new potatoes

225 g/8 oz cauliflower

225 g/8 oz button mushrooms

1 large onion

3 carrots

6 tbsp ghee or vegetable oil

2 garlic cloves, crushed

4 tsp chopped ginger

1–2 fresh green chillies, deseeded and chopped

1 tbsp paprika

2 tsp ground coriander

1 tbsp mild or medium curry powder

450 ml/16 fl oz vegetable stock

400 g/14 oz canned chopped tomatoes

1 green pepper, deseeded and sliced

1 tbsp cornflour

150 ml/5 fl oz coconut milk

salt

fresh coriander sprigs, to garnish

Cut the aubergine, turnips and potatoes into 1-cm/½-inch cubes. Break the cauliflower into small florets. Leave the mushrooms whole if small or slice them thickly, if preferred. Slice the onion and carrots.

Heat the ghee in a large saucepan over a low heat. Add the onion, turnips, potatoes and cauliflower and cook, stirring frequently, for 3 minutes.

Add the garlic, ginger, chilli, paprika, ground coriander and curry powder and cook, stirring constantly, for 1 minute.

Add the stock, tomatoes, aubergine and mushrooms and season to taste with salt. Cover and simmer, stirring occasionally, for 30 minutes, or until tender. Add the green pepper and carrots, cover and cook for a further 5 minutes.

Put the cornflour and coconut milk in a bowl, mix into a smooth paste and stir into the vegetable mixture. Simmer, stirring constantly, for 2 minutes. Taste and adjust the seasoning, if necessary. Transfer to serving bowls, garnish with coriander sprigs and serve at once with freshly cooked rice.

Onion, Potato & Red Pepper Curry

serves 4

2 tbsp vegetable or groundnut oil

2 red onions, sliced

2 garlic cloves, finely chopped

5-cm/2-inch piece fresh ginger, finely chopped

1 red chilli, deseeded and chopped

1 tbsp Thai red curry paste

225 g/8 oz potatoes, cut into cubes, boiled for 5 minutes and drained

2 red peppers, deseeded and diced

300 ml/10 fl oz vegetable stock

1 tsp salt

4 tbsp chopped fresh coriander

Heat the oil in a wok or large frying pan and stir-fry the onions, garlic, ginger and chilli for 2–3 minutes. Add the curry paste and stir-fry over a low heat for 2–3 minutes. Add the potatoes, peppers, stock and salt and cook for 3–4 minutes, or until all the vegetables are tender. Stir in the coriander and serve immediately.

4

Side
Dishes

Garlic Mash

serves 4

900 g/2 lb floury potatoes, cut into chunks

8 garlic cloves, crushed

150 ml/5 fl oz milk

85 g/3 oz butter

pinch of freshly grated nutmeg

salt and pepper

Place the potatoes in a large saucepan with enough water to cover and a pinch of salt. Bring to the boil and cook for 10 minutes. Add the garlic and cook for a further 10–15 minutes, or until the potatoes are tender.

Drain the potatoes and garlic, reserving 3 tablespoons of the cooking liquid. Return the reserved cooking liquid to the saucepan, then add the milk and bring to simmering point. Add the butter, return the potatoes and garlic to the saucepan and turn off the heat. Mash thoroughly with a potato masher.

Season the potato mixture to taste with nutmeg, salt and pepper and beat thoroughly with a wooden spoon until light and fluffy. Serve immediately.

Roasted Potato Wedges with Shallots & Rosemary

serves 4

1 kg/2 lb 4 oz small old potatoes

6 tbsp Spanish olive oil

2 sprigs fresh rosemary

150 g/5½ oz baby shallots

2 garlic cloves, sliced

salt and pepper

Preheat the oven to 200°C/400°F/Gas Mark 6. Peel and cut each potato into 8 thick wedges. Put the potatoes in a large saucepan of lightly salted water and bring to the boil. Reduce the heat and simmer for 5 minutes.

Heat the oil in a large roasting tin. Drain the potatoes well and add to the roasting tin. Strip the leaves from the rosemary sprigs, chop finely and sprinkle over the potatoes.

Roast the potatoes in the preheated oven for 35 minutes, turning twice during cooking. Add the shallots and garlic and roast for a further 15 minutes until golden brown. Season to taste with salt and pepper.

Transfer to a warmed serving dish and serve hot.

Warm Potatoes with Pesto

serves 4

450 g/1 lb small new potatoes

3 tsp pesto

25 g/1 oz Parmesan cheese, grated

salt and pepper

Bring a large saucepan of salted water to the boil. Add the potatoes and cook for 15 minutes, or until tender. Drain, transfer to a salad bowl and leave to cool slightly.

Add the pesto and salt and pepper to taste and toss together. Sprinkle with the Parmesan cheese and serve warm.

Perfect Roast Potatoes

serves 6

1.3 kg/3 lb large, floury potatoes, such as King Edward, Maris Piper or Desirée, peeled and cut into even-sized chunks

3 tbsp olive oil

salt

Preheat the oven to 220°C/425°F/Gas Mark 7. Bring a large saucepan of salted water to the boil, add the potatoes and cook, covered, for 5–7 minutes. They will still be firm. Remove from the heat.

Meanwhile, put the oil in a roasting tin and heat in the preheated oven.

Drain the potatoes well and return to the saucepan. Cover with the lid and firmly shake the saucepan so that the surface of the potatoes is roughened, to help give a much crisper texture.

Remove the roasting tin from the oven and carefully tip the potatoes into the hot oil. Baste to ensure that they are all well coated with the oil.

Roast at the top of the preheated oven for 45–50 minutes until the potatoes are browned all over and thoroughly crisp, turning only once halfway through the cooking time and basting, otherwise the crunchy edges will be destroyed.

Carefully transfer the potatoes to a warmed serving dish. Sprinkle with a little salt and serve at once.

Chilli Roast Potatoes

serves 4

500 g/1 lb 2 oz small new
potatoes, scrubbed

150 ml/5 fl oz vegetable oil

1 tsp chilli powder

½ tsp caraway seeds

1 tsp salt

1 tbsp fresh basil, shredded

Cook the potatoes in a saucepan of boiling water for 10 minutes, then drain thoroughly.

Pour a little of the oil into a shallow roasting tin to coat the base. Heat the oil in a preheated oven, 200°C/400°F/ Gas Mark 6, for 10 minutes. Add the potatoes to the tin and brush them with the hot oil.

In a small bowl, mix together the chilli powder, caraway seeds and salt. Sprinkle the mixture over the potatoes, turning to coat them all over.

Add the remaining oil to the tin and roast in the oven for about 15 minutes, or until the potatoes are cooked through.

Using a slotted spoon, remove the potatoes from the the oil, draining them thoroughly, and transfer them to a warmed serving dish. Sprinkle the shredded basil over the top and serve immediately.

Caramelized Sweet Potatoes

serves 4

450 g/1 lb sweet potatoes

55 g/2 oz butter, plus extra for greasing

55 g/2 oz brown sugar, maple syrup or honey

2 tbsp orange or pineapple juice

55 g/2 oz pineapple pieces (optional)

pinch of ground cinnamon, nutmeg or mixed spice (optional)

Scrub the sweet potatoes, but do not peel. Bring a large saucepan of salted water to the boil. Add the sweet potatoes and cook for 30–45 minutes, depending on their size, until just tender. Remove from the heat and drain well. Leave to cool slightly, then peel.

Preheat the oven to 200°C/400°F/Gas Mark 6. Thickly slice the sweet potatoes and arrange in a single overlapping layer in a greased ovenproof dish. Cut the butter into small cubes and dot over the top.

Sprinkle with the sugar and fruit juice. Add the pineapple and spices, if using.

Bake in the preheated oven, basting occasionally, for 30–40 minutes until golden brown. Serve hot.

Potato-topped Vegetables

serves 4

1 carrot, diced

175 g/6 oz cauliflower florets

175 g/6 oz broccoli florets

1 fennel bulb, sliced

85 g/3 oz French beans, halved

25 g/1 oz butter

25 g/1 oz plain flour

150 ml/5 fl oz vegetable stock

150 ml/5 fl oz dry white wine

150 ml/5 fl oz milk

175 g/6 oz chestnut mushrooms, quartered

2 tbsp chopped fresh sage

topping

900 g/2 lb floury potatoes, diced

25 g/1 oz butter

4 tbsp natural yogurt

70 g/2½ oz Parmesan cheese, grated

1 tsp fennel seeds

salt and pepper

Preheat the oven to 190°C/375°F/Gas Mark 5. Bring a large saucepan of water to the boil, add the carrot, cauliflower, broccoli, fennel and beans and cook for 10 minutes, or until just tender. Drain and set aside.

Melt the butter in a saucepan over a low heat, add the flour and cook, stirring constantly, for 1 minute. Remove from the heat and stir in the stock, wine and milk. Return to the heat, bring to the boil and cook, stirring constantly, until thickened. Stir in the reserved vegetables, mushrooms and sage.

To make the topping, bring a large saucepan of water to the boil, add the potatoes and cook for 10–15 minutes until tender. Drain, return to the saucepan and add the butter, yogurt and half the cheese. Mash with a potato masher or a fork. Stir in the fennel seeds and salt and pepper to taste.

Spoon the vegetable mixture into a 1-litre/1¾-pint pie dish. Top with the potato mixture. Sprinkle over the remaining cheese. Bake in the preheated oven for 30–35 minutes until golden. Serve at once.

Sweet Potato Salad with Green Olives

serves 4–6

3 tbsp olive or argan oil

1 red onion, roughly chopped

25 g/1 oz fresh ginger, peeled and grated

1 tsp cumin seeds

450 g/1 lb orange sweet potatoes, peeled and cut into bite-sized cubes

½ tsp paprika

8–10 green olives

rind of ½ preserved lemon, finely chopped

juice of ½ lemon

1 small bunch fresh flat-leaf parsley, finely chopped

1 small bunch fresh coriander, finely chopped

salt and pepper

Heat 2 tablespoons of the oil in a tagine or heavy-based, flameproof casserole, add the onion and cook over a medium heat for 2–3 minutes, stirring frequently, until it begins to colour. Add the ginger and cumin seeds and cook for 1–2 minutes, stirring, until fragrant.

Toss in the sweet potatoes along with the paprika and the remaining oil. Season to taste with salt and pepper and pour in just enough water to cover the base of the tagine or casserole. Cover and cook gently for 10 minutes, or until the sweet potato is tender but firm and the liquid has reduced.

Toss in the olives and preserved lemon rind and refresh with the lemon juice. Serve warm or at room temperature, with the parsley and coriander scattered over.

Potato Salad

serves 4

700 g/1 lb 9 oz tiny new potatoes

8 spring onions

1 hard-boiled egg (optional)

250 ml/9 fl oz low-fat mayonnaise

1 tsp paprika

salt and pepper

2 tbsp snipped chives and a pinch of paprika

Bring a large pan of lightly salted water to the boil. Add the new potatoes to the pan and cook for 10–15 minutes, or until they are just tender.

Drain the potatoes in a colander and rinse them under cold running water until they are completely cold. Drain them again thoroughly. Transfer the potatoes to a mixing bowl and leave until required.

Trim and slice the spring onions thinly on the diagonal. Chop the hard-boiled egg, if using.

Mix together the mayonnaise, paprika, and salt and pepper to taste in a bowl until well blended. Pour the mixture over the potatoes.

Add the sliced spring onions and egg, if using, to the potatoes and toss together.

Transfer the potato salad to a serving bowl, sprinkle with snipped chives and a pinch of paprika. Cover with clingfilm and chill in the refrigerator until required.

Potato, Rocket & Apple Salad

serves 4

600 g/1 lb 5 oz potatoes, unpeeled and sliced

2 green eating apples, cored and diced

1 tsp lemon juice

25 g/1 oz walnut pieces

125 g/4½ oz goat's cheese, diced

150 g/5½ oz rocket leaves

salt and pepper

dressing

2 tbsp olive oil

1 tbsp red wine vinegar

1 tsp clear honey

1 tsp fennel seeds

Cook the potatoes in a large pan of boiling water for 15 minutes until tender. Drain and leave to cool. Transfer the cooled potatoes to a serving bowl.

Toss the diced apples in the lemon juice, then drain and stir them into the cold potatoes.

Add the walnut pieces, cheese cubes and rocket leaves, then toss the ingredients together to mix.

In a small bowl or jug, whisk all of the dressing ingredients together and then pour the dressing over the salad. Season to taste and serve immediately.

Mexican Potato Salad

serves 4

1.25 kg/2 lb 12 oz waxy
potatoes, sliced

1 ripe avocado

1 tsp olive oil

1 tsp lemon juice

1 garlic clove, crushed

1 onion, chopped

2 large tomatoes, sliced

1 fresh green chilli,
deseeded and chopped

1 yellow pepper, deseeded
and sliced

2 tbsp chopped fresh
coriander

salt and pepper

lime or lemon wedges,
to garnish

Cook the potato slices in a saucepan of boiling water for
10–15 minutes, or until tender. Drain and leave to cool.

Meanwhile, cut the avocado in half, remove the stone and
peel. Mash the avocado flesh with a fork (you could also
scoop the avocado flesh from the 2 halves using a spoon
and then mash it).

Add the olive oil, lemon juice, garlic and onion to the
avocado flesh and stir to mix. Cover the bowl with clingfilm,
to minimize discoloration, and reserve.

Mix the tomatoes, chilli and yellow pepper together and
transfer to a salad bowl with the potato slices.

Arrange the avocado mixture on top of the salad and sprinkle
with the chopped coriander. Season to taste with salt and
pepper and serve immediately, garnished with lime wedges.

Potatoes in Red Wine

serves 4

125 g/4½ oz butter

450 g/1 lb new potatoes, halved

200 ml/7 fl oz red wine

6 tbsp beef stock

8 shallots, halved

125 g/4½ oz oyster mushrooms

1 tbsp chopped fresh sage or coriander

salt and pepper

fresh sage leaves or coriander sprigs, to garnish

Melt the butter in a heavy-based frying pan and add the potatoes. Cook over a low heat for 5 minutes, stirring constantly.

Add the red wine, beef stock and shallots. Season to taste with salt and pepper and simmer for 30 minutes.

Stir in the mushrooms and chopped herbs and cook for 5 minutes.

Turn the potatoes and mushrooms into a warm serving dish. Garnish with fresh sage leaves and serve at once.

Potatoes Dauphinois

serves 4

1 tbsp butter

675 g/1½ lb waxy potatoes, sliced

2 garlic cloves, crushed

1 red onion, sliced

85 g/3 oz Gruyère cheese, grated

300 ml/10 fl oz double cream

salt and pepper

Lightly grease a 1-litre/1¾-pint shallow ovenproof dish with the butter.

Arrange a single layer of potato slices evenly in the base of the prepared dish.

Top the potato slices with half the garlic, half the sliced red onion and one third of the grated Gruyère cheese. Season to taste with a little salt and some pepper.

Repeat the layers in exactly the same order, finishing with a layer of potatoes topped with grated cheese.

Pour the cream over the top of the potatoes and cook in a preheated oven, 180°C/350°F/Gas Mark 4, for 1½ hours, or until the potatoes are cooked through and the top is browned and crispy. Serve at once, straight from the dish.

Garlic & Chilli-flavoured Potatoes with Cauliflower

serves 4

350 g/12 oz new potatoes

1 small cauliflower

2 tbsp sunflower or olive oil

1 tsp black or brown mustard seeds

1 tsp cumin seeds

5 large garlic cloves, lightly crushed, then chopped

1–2 green chillies, finely chopped (deseeded if you like)

½ tsp ground turmeric

½ tsp salt, or to taste

2 tbsp chopped fresh coriander leaves

Cook the potatoes in their skins in a saucepan of boiling water for 20 minutes, or until tender. Drain, then soak in cold water for 30 minutes. Peel them, if you like, then halve or quarter according to their size – they should be only slightly bigger than the cauliflower florets.

Meanwhile, divide the cauliflower into about 1-cm/½-inch diameter florets and blanch in a large saucepan of boiling salted water for 3 minutes. Drain and plunge into iced water to prevent further cooking, then drain again.

Heat the oil in a medium-sized saucepan over a medium heat. When hot but not smoking, add the mustard seeds, then the cumin seeds.

Remove from the heat and add the garlic and chillies. Return to a low heat and cook, stirring, until the garlic has a light brown tinge.

Stir in the turmeric, followed by the cauliflower and the potatoes. Add the salt, increase the heat slightly and cook, stirring, until the vegetables are well blended with the spices and heated through.

Stir in the coriander, remove from the heat and serve immediately to accompany any Indian main course dish.

Home-made Oven Chips

serves 4

450 g/1 lb potatoes

2 tbsp sunflower oil

salt and pepper

Preheat the oven to 200°C/400°F/Gas Mark 6.

Cut the potatoes into thick, even-sized chips. Rinse them under cold running water and then dry well on a clean tea towel. Put in a bowl, add the oil and toss together until coated.

Spread the chips on a baking sheet and cook in the oven for 40–45 minutes, turning once, until golden. Add salt and pepper to taste and serve hot.

Spicy Potato Chips

serves 4

4 large waxy potatoes

2 sweet potatoes

4 tbsp butter, melted

½ tsp chilli powder

1 tsp garam masala

salt

Cut both the potatoes and sweet potatoes into slices about 1 cm/½ inch thick, then cut them into finger-shaped chips.

Place the potatoes in a large bowl of cold salted water. Leave to soak for 20 minutes.

Remove the potato slices with a slotted spoon and drain thoroughly. Pat with kitchen paper until they are completely dry.

Pour the melted butter on to a baking tray. Transfer the potato slices to the baking tray.

Sprinkle with the chilli powder and garam masala, turning the potato slices to coat them with the spice mixture.

Cook the chips in a preheated oven, 200°C/400°F/Gas Mark 6, turning frequently, for 40 minutes, until browned and cooked through.

Drain the chips well on kitchen paper to remove the excess oil and serve immediately.

Garlic Potato Wedges

serves 4

3 large baking potatoes, scrubbed

4 tbsp olive oil

2 tbsp butter

2 garlic cloves, chopped

1 tbsp chopped fresh rosemary

1 tbsp chopped fresh parsley

1 tbsp chopped fresh thyme

salt and pepper

Bring a large pan of water to the boil, add the potatoes and parboil them for 10 minutes. Drain the potatoes, refresh under cold water and then drain them again thoroughly.

Transfer the potatoes to a chopping board. When the potatoes are cold enough to handle, cut them into thick wedges, but do not peel.

Preheat the grill. Heat the oil and butter in a small pan together with the garlic. Cook gently until the garlic begins to brown, then remove the pan from the heat.

Stir the herbs and seasoning into the mixture in the pan.

Brush the herb and butter mixture all over the potato wedges.

Cook under the grill for 10-15 minutes or until the potato wedges are just tender, brushing liberally with any of the remaining herb and butter mixture.

Transfer the garlic potato wedges to a warmed serving plate and serve.

Paprika Crisps

serves 4

2 large potatoes

3 tbsp olive oil

½ tsp paprika

salt

Slice the potatoes very thinly so that they are almost transparent and place in a bowl of cold water, then drain them thoroughly and pat dry with kitchen paper.

Heat the oil in a large, heavy-based frying pan and add the paprika. Cook, stirring constantly to ensure that the paprika doesn't catch on the base and burn.

Preheat the grill. Add the potato slices to the frying pan and cook them in a single layer over a medium-low heat for about 5 minutes, or until the potato slices are just beginning to curl slightly at the edges.

Remove the potato slices from the pan using a slotted spoon and transfer them to kitchen paper to drain thoroughly.

Sprinkle the potato slices with salt and cook under a medium grill, turning frequently, for 10 minutes, until they begin to go crisp. Sprinkle with a little more salt and serve immediately.